Published in 2022 by Orange Mosquito
An Imprint of Welbeck Children's Limited
part of Welbeck Publishing Group.
Based in London and Sydney.
www.welbeckpublishing.com

In collaboration with Mosquito Books Barcelona S.L.

© Mosquito Books Barcelona, SL 2021
Text © Anna Omedes 2021
Illustration © Laura Fraile 2021
Translation: Catalina Girona
Publisher: Margaux Durigon
UK editor: Jo Hanks
Production: Jess Brisley

ISBN: 9781914519246
eISBN: 9781914519253

Printed in China
10 9 8 7 6 5 4 3 2 1

FSC
MIX
Paper
FSC® C020056

COLORFUL KINGDOM

How animals use color to surprise and survive

ANNA OMEDES • LAURA FRAILE

ORANGE
M·O·S·Q·U·I·T·O

STORIES

THEATRICAL ARCHITECTURE 28

BEING THE CENTRE OF ATTENTION 30

COLORS YOU CAN EAT 32

SHINING WITH THEIR OWN LIGHT 34

METAMORPHOSIS IN COLORS 36

LOOK AT MY PRETTY LEGS! 38

HOW DOES IT CHANGE COLORS? 40

YUCK! HOW DISGUSTING! 42

BLUE, AN OPTICAL ILLUSION 44

The species are not shown here in proportion to their respective sizes in real life.

A MYRIAD OF COLORS

Colors have many uses for living creatures. Animals use them, for instance, to show their power within a group, find a mate, hide from their predators or hunt without being seen.

Many millions of years ago, there were not a lot of colors in nature, but it didn't matter much because many animals' eyes were incapable of seeing them anyway. Animals' increased perception of colors are an extraordinary outcome of the gradual evolution of the animal kingdom.

With great scientific rigor, this book reveals how animals of all kinds – from different parts of the world – use color to survive and evolve as a species in their natural habitats.

But where do colors come from?

Some colors in nature are from the pigments that exist in us; others are produced via optical effects that combine with these natural colors.

Pigments

Biological pigments are colored substances produced by living beings. It is thanks to them that nature attains the wealth and splendor of colors we can see in plants and animals.

Melanin

Practically all living beings produce their own melanin, which is the most abundant pigment in nature. There are two types of melanin: eumelanin, which produces black and brown tones, and pheomelanin, responsible for reddish and orange hues.

Carotenoids

Carotenoid pigments produce yellows, oranges, pinks and reds. Only plants, algae, fungi and bacteria can synthesize (form) them, which means that all animals (including humans) have to obtain these colors through food.

The crab spider changes its colors to catch insects by blending in with the flowers in its hunting ground. When yellow flowers bloom, the spider releases a yellow pigment in its skin; when white flowers start blossoming, it eliminates the yellow pigment and turns white in just a few days.

Black hair contains 99% eumelanin and only 1% pheomelanin; brown hair has 5% pheomelanin and redheads have up to 33% pheomelanin in their hair. White hair is hair devoid of melanin.

Not all of us see the same

Not all animals have the same quality of sight: some have excellent vision and others are nearly blind. Some birds have vision five times sharper than ours and can spot small objects from hundreds of yards away. There are animals, above all insects and birds, that can even see ultraviolet light, which we cannot. Seeing colors depends on how many types of receptors the eyes have. For instance, the human eye has three types which can see green, red and blue and their combinations. But deer only have two, so, unfortunately for them, they cannot distinguish well between the color of the tiger and the vegetation behind which it is hiding.

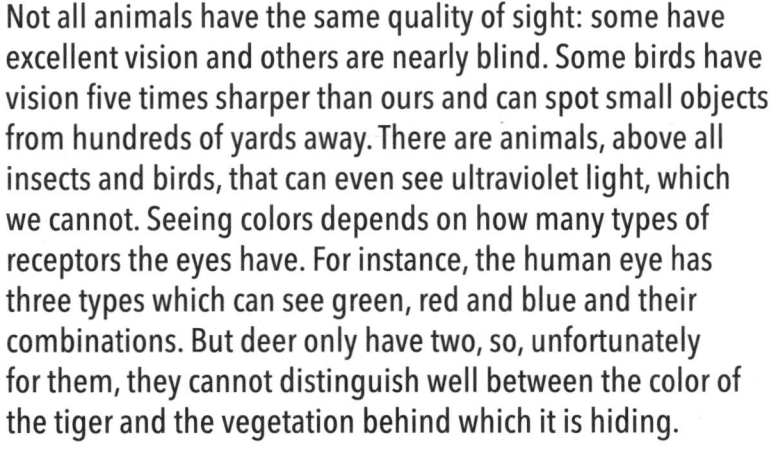

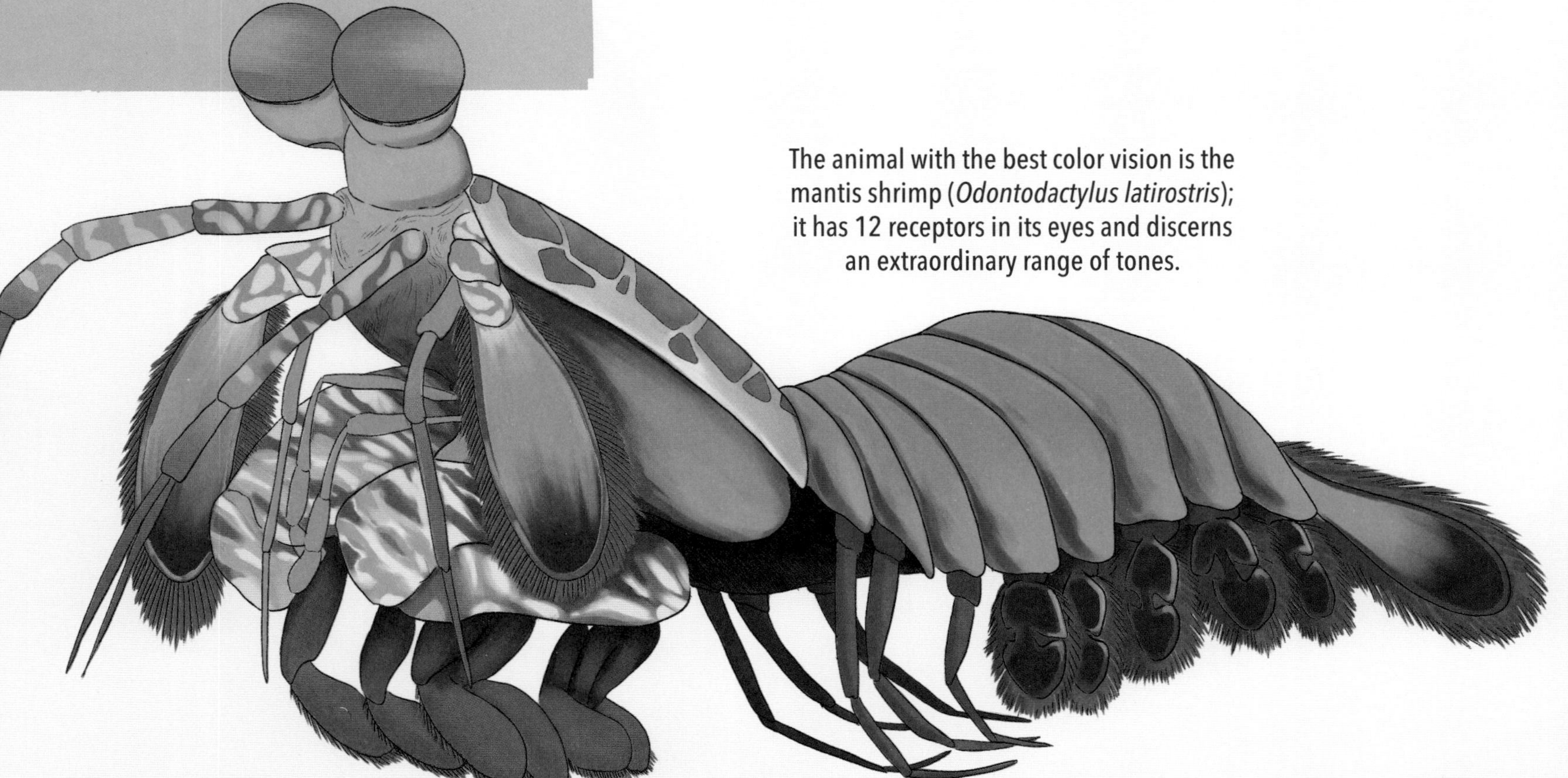

The animal with the best color vision is the mantis shrimp (*Odontodactylus latirostris*); it has 12 receptors in its eyes and discerns an extraordinary range of tones.

LEADER OF THE TROOP

Mandrill
Mandrillus sphinx
Cameroon, Equatorial Guinea, Congo, Gabon and Nigeria

The male mandrill is the most colorful mammal in the world. Mandrills live in tropical forests in large groups of 600-800 individuals called hordes. They are omnivores and travel on the ground, sleeping high in trees in a different place each day. The males' colorings increase with age and show their individual position within the social hierarchy. The more colors on the face and rump, the higher the individual's social rank. The leader of the herd is the male with the greatest number of colors and the most vivid ones. The males defend their status through frequent fights, some of them deadly. The females prefer to mate with dominant males, ensuring the health of their offspring and the father's protection, especially against their main predator – the leopard.

Where do mandrills get their colors?

Most mammals are black or brown, because their mane or fur only contains two pigments: eumelanin (black-brown) and pheomelanin (red-yellow). Their skin does not contain vivid-colored pigments either, not even in the mandrill. A mandrill's colors appear through the dispersal of light in the collagen fibers of their face and rump. The mandrill's colorfulness is stimulated by testosterone (the main male sex hormone) which females also produce, although in smaller quantities. For this reason, during the mating season, the colors of both males and females grow in intensity.

I'm the boss here

It looks like the 'leader of the pack', or in this case, the troop, is angry because a younger male has challenged him. All he has to do is show his colors and bare his fangs for the younger mandrill to give up and move away.

There are some 50,000 species of spider in the world; most of them have extremely poor eyesight and can distinguish very few colors. Surprisingly, however, the 6,000 species of the jumping spider family have some of the best vision not only among arachnids but all arthropods (invertebrates with jointed legs like insects or crustaceans). The peacock spider, with its eight eyes, belongs to this group.

THE SPIDER'S DANCE

Peacock spiders
Maratus
Australia and Tasmania

Peacock spiders are very small, measuring around 0.2 inches in length. Their name comes from the vivid colors on the males' abdomens, which they exhibit during courtship, just as peacocks do with their tail feathers.

Brilliant blues, greens, oranges and yellows combine in highly spectacular geometrical patterns to impress potential mates, as well as other males in ritual exhibition contests. The females, on the other hand, are compact and inconspicuous, being white or gray with dark brown patches. The male carries out an elaborate courtship dance before the female, displaying his colorful abdomen, strutting from one side to another and rhythmically stretching out his legs. Each species has its own dance, and its precise execution reassures the female that this is the mate for her. If she enjoys the dance, the male will have succeeded. But if the male doesn't dance properly, the female rejects him – and may even see him as prey and devour him. This system ensures that fertilization occurs exclusively between pairs of the same species.

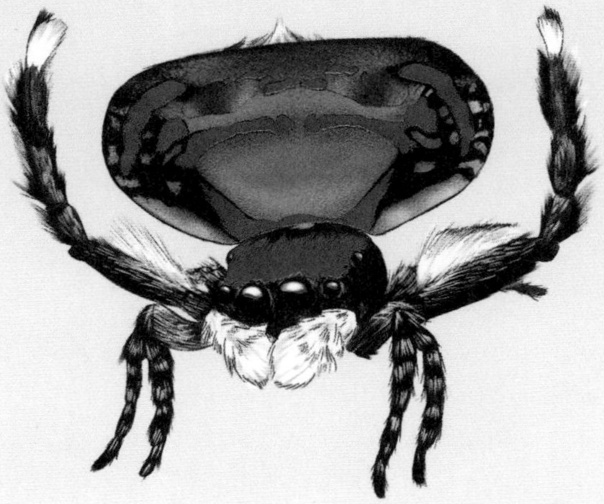

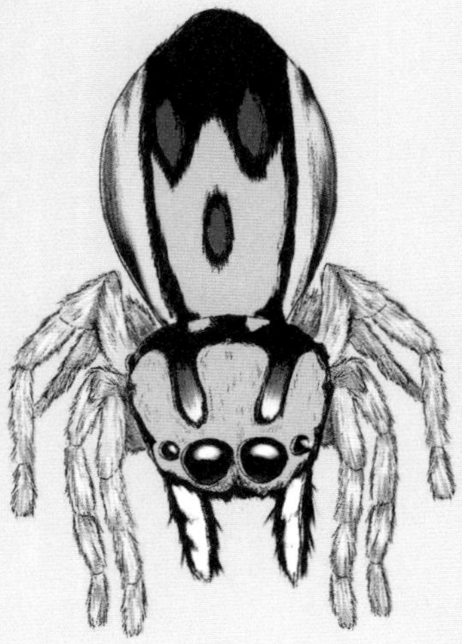

The dangers of love

This male is trying to woo the female with his courtship dance, moving his abdomen and legs in rhythm. This dance, as well as the male's color pattern, are unique to the peacock spider species.

Some males dance better than others, and we hope this one does well. If the female enjoys his performance, she will allow him to fertilize her.

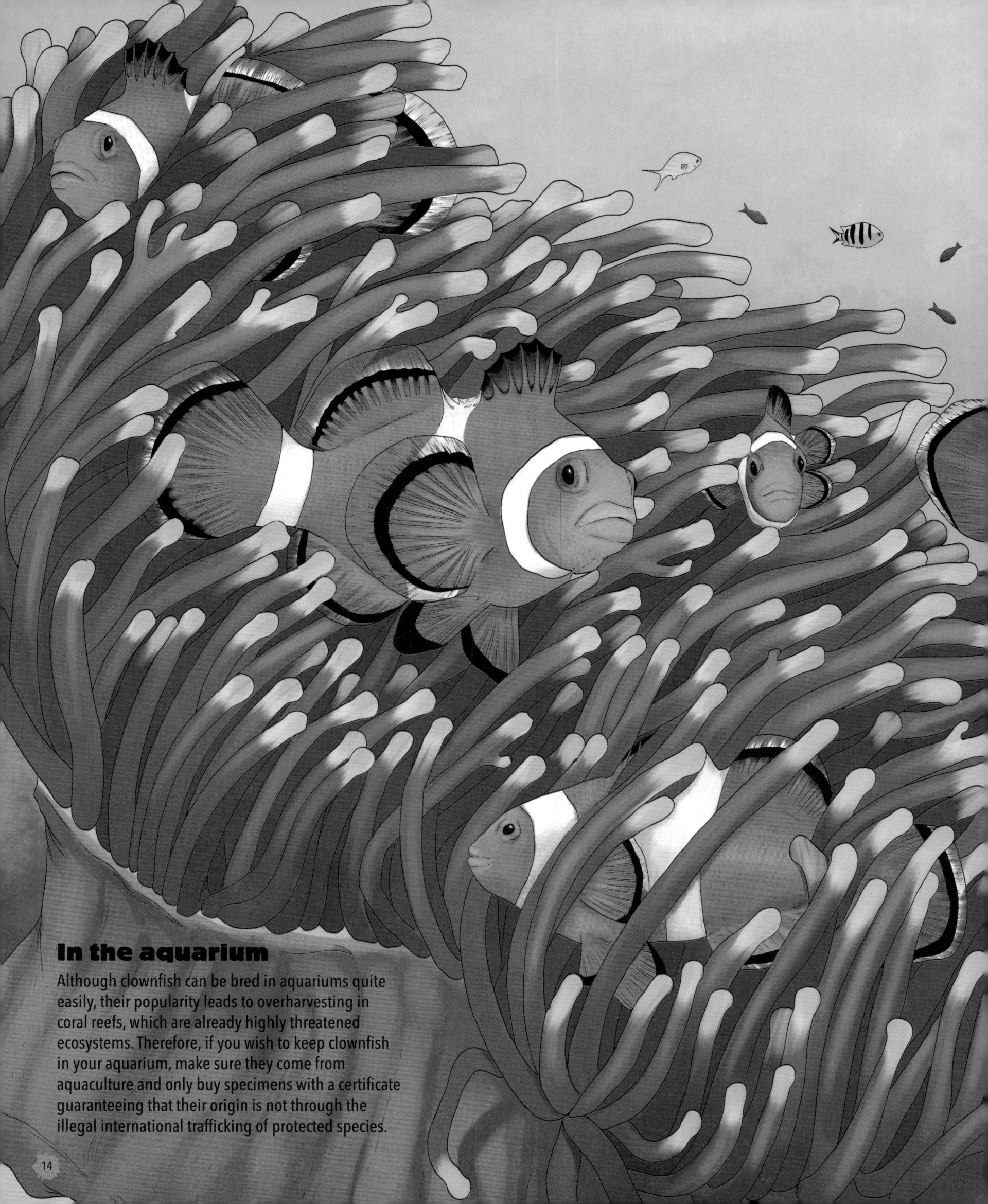

In the aquarium

Although clownfish can be bred in aquariums quite easily, their popularity leads to overharvesting in coral reefs, which are already highly threatened ecosystems. Therefore, if you wish to keep clownfish in your aquarium, make sure they come from aquaculture and only buy specimens with a certificate guaranteeing that their origin is not through the illegal international trafficking of protected species.

I'll help you if you help me

Clownfish eat leftover particles from the anemone's diet and in return, continually clean their tentacles and mouths to free the anemone from annoying parasites. In addition, as clownfish are constantly swimming and flapping their fins, they increase the flow of water that brings in small fish and other organisms that the anemone can catch. Not only that, but clownfish also defend their anemones from certain specialized predators that attack them, such as butterflyfish.

LIVING IN HARMONY

Common clownfish
Amphiprion ocellaris
Tropical coral reefs in the Indian and Pacific Oceans

Clownfish are brightly colored so that individuals of the 30 existing species can recognize one another. They live in the coral reefs of tropical waters and have developed a symbiotic (interdependent) relationship with the sea anemones that inhabit the same ecosystems. Anemones live fixed on rocks and have highly toxic stinging tentacles that they use to capture the small animals on which they feed. These dangerous appendages deter many species from getting too close to them; however, clownfish have evolved a resistance to anemone toxin and exploit this for their own protection. Clownfish are not very good swimmers and they would be easy prey for predators in open water; anemones offer them protection and shelter. When born, clownfish are not immune to the anemone's poison, but as they grow older they gradually acquire a resistance. The adult fish live in constant contact with anemone's tentacles for the rest of their lives, which is from six to 10 years!

SEEING WITHOUT BEING SEEN

Tiger

Panthera tigris

Various parts of Asia.

Camouflage is a technique used by many animal species. It consists of concealing one's body in the environment; whether in the lush foliage of jungles, in vast savannahs, in rugged rocky areas, in ice and snow or on seabeds. Animals camouflage themselves for two different reasons: to avoid being seen by predators, so that they will not be attacked; or to stalk their prey without being discovered. The tiger is a large predator and fears virtually no animal. It uses camouflage to hunt.

The most hunted feline

Because of their size, the tiger and the lion are kings of the felines. But it is the tiger, because of its beauty, harmonious movements, solitary nature and ferocity, that is the most legendary in the cultures of the areas where it has lived. There are six subspecies of tiger, the most numerous being the Bengal tiger (Panthera tigris tigris). All are endangered, mainly because of humans: poachers kill them to sell their skins, claws and teeth, as well as other body parts used in traditional and alternative medicine in some countries. In 1900 there were approximately 100,000 tigers in the wild, today it is estimated that there are only about 4,000. In addition, there are some 20,000 tigers held in captivity in zoos around the world.

Fooling the eye

Tigers have dark vertical stripes that stand out against their tawny fur. This color combination allows them to go unnoticed among many types of vegetation and also in the rocky areas of the mountains where some subspecies live. As a result, they can sneak up on their prey, getting much closer before pouncing on it. The coloring of tigers is individual: each has its own pattern of dark stripes, although from a distance it may look the same as other tigers.

Solid, striped or spotted?

Today there are 37 species of felines. Evolution over thousands and thousands of years has determined that their coats be differentiated into four basic types: solid (lion), striped (tiger), rosettes (jaguar) or spotted (cheetah). Scientists believe that the oldest pattern is the spotted one and that the others are derived from it.

SEEKING A PARTNER

Great tit
Parus major
Europe, Asia and Africa.

In general, male birds with the most conspicuous feathers are better at getting food and defending the nest - traits associated with being good parents. But as attractive as they may be, male birds are not usually the ones deciding who to mate with. The truth is that when the mating period arrives, it is the females who choose their mates after carefully observing the displays put on by the different candidates.

Finding the balance

The chest of the male great tit is bright yellow, with a black area on it called a bib, which extends down between the legs and reaches to the base of the tail. The yellow feathers get their beautiful color from pigments found mainly in the caterpillars on which it feeds. A bright yellow color indicates that the bird has eaten a lot of caterpillars, and it is a very skillful hunter. The size of the male's black bib indicates his dominance: the larger the bib, the fiercer he is, indicating that he will be highly capable of defending the nest and its contents. Generally, female great tits prefer to mate with a balanced male: one that is a good hunter so he can feed their chicks and dominant enough to defend them; but not one that wastes a lot of time fighting with other males.

Eating colors

The seductive power of the colors in many birds has a biological explanation. To obtain them, it is necessary to eat the pigments that will later be reproduced in the feathers. The most sought-after colors are red, yellow and orange; hues that birds obtain by consuming carotenoids (pigments that are present in plants and algae). This is why bright and luminous colors in birds are indicative of good health and survivability.

19

POISONOUS FROGS

Poison dart frogs
Dendrobatidae
Central and South America

Poison dart frogs are also called poison arrow frogs. These names derive from the fact that most species have a toxic alkaloid in their skin, which locals have always used to poison their hunting darts and arrows. All species exhibit highly striking, varied coloring that is unique in nature. They live mainly in the humid, lush rainforests of Panama and Costa Rica and in the forests of the Colombian Andes.

Danger signs

Aposematism is the use of warning coloration to prevent attack by predators. It works in the opposite way to camouflage, but has one of the same objectives: to avoid being eaten. In this case, it's not about going unnoticed, but rather being as visible as possible. This is where the poison arrow frogs' bright colors and fantastic patterns come in handy. Although all poison arrow frogs have some poison in their skin, they are not all equally dangerous. The poison of the golden frog (*Phyllobates terribilis*) is 20 times stronger than the curare (a plant-based poison) used by indigenous Amazonians; even a small dose would kill a person instantly. Others, in contrast, are not very poisonous, but take advantage of the fact that bright colors instill fear in potential attackers, who avoid eating any highly colorful frogs just in case.

If you eat me, you're dead

These Central and South American venomous frogs are very small. The largest species reach up to over 2 inches in length, but some are tiny and grow no more than about 0.79 inch long. That means they are an attractive morsel that would be easy for many predators to catch, from birds to snakes and spiders. But their pretty colors are a dead giveaway of the dangerous poison they harbor. Over thousands of years, predatory species have learned that eating a tasty, beautifully-colored frog can have very negative consequences, even death.

THE MYSTERIOUS CUTTLEFISH

Australian giant cuttlefish
Sepia apama
Australian reefs

Cuttlefish have long fascinated scientists and amateur observers alike. They are capable of changing their colors as often as they like and in a matter of seconds. They can also alter the texture of their skin from a smooth, shiny surface to a dull, wrinkled one, full of warty bumps. This allows them to camouflage themselves quickly, blending in with rocky seafloors, sand or algae. By constantly moving the colors on their skin, cuttlefish give the appearance of swimming backwards. They can also create two large, false eyes on their back so that predators think they are a much larger animal and pass them by. Cuttlefish are extraordinary and remain a mystery to science.

Instant change of disguise

Of all the cuttlefish species, the Australian giant cuttlefish is the largest in the world. It grows up to twenty inches long and can weigh more than 22 pounds. In less than a second, it transforms from being perfectly camouflaged among algae in order to fool a predator, to sporting a brightly-colored coat to attract a potential mate.

Chromatophores

Cuttlefish have skin covered with chromatophores, special cells containing different pigments that can change size at will. Using part of their musculature, they contract some muscles to display light-dotted patterns or expand them to produce large dark spots. Thanks to this resource, the number of designs they create is truly unique in nature. Sometimes the patterns are not fixed, but are in continuous movement. When they feel attacked, cuttlefish mimic their surroundings so as not to be seen. And during mating rituals, males and females are constantly 'dancing', changing their colors and exchanging messages through these patterns.

Colorful females

Generally, in bird species where the male is very brightly colored, it is the female (who tends to be discreetly colored) that chooses the mate. It is curious that female Gouldian finches are also brightly colored, even if they do not reach the brightness of the males. Perhaps this is why males in this species tend to do the choosing of their mates (and show a preference for more colorful females).

Saving the nest

Gouldian finches are monogamous and mate for life. They usually form large flocks of up to 1,000 individuals, together with other finch species. When the breeding season arrives, pairs choose a hole in a tree to build a nest, and after the eggs are laid, they take turns brooding them. When a predator appears, the male moves away from the nest and maneuvers ostentatiously in the air, displaying his colors to attract its attention. He thus distracts the predator, risking his life, to lead it away from the female and chicks.

A COLORFUL BIRD

Gouldian finch
Erythrura gouldiae
Northern Australia

There are few birds in the world as striking as the Gouldian finch, also known as the rainbow finch. They are very brightly colored, especially the males. All Gouldian finches have green upper bodies, a lilac breast and a bright yellow belly, and sports a beautiful turquoise collar. In the wild, the species has three color variants on the head: black (most abundant), red and orange (very rare). This spectacular coloring is the reason why these finches are widely bred in captivity for sale as pets. The species is classified as near-threatened with extinction, with an estimated 2,500 individuals remaining in the wild in Australia. Trapping and export are now banned: in the 1950s some 11,000 birds were captured annually; in the 1981 season, the last in which trappers were licensed, more than 1,000 were caught.

COLORS FOR DECEIVING

False coral snake
Oxyrhopus petolarius
True coral snake
Micrurus annelatus

Central America and northern South America

The bite of the true coral snake is very dangerous, since its venom can be deadly for many animals as well as humans. Its colorful rings warn potential predators they had better watch out. However, there are some snake species that mimic the color patterns of coral snakes in order to ward off potential attackers, often other snakes. The venom of the so-called false coral snake is not very potent and is only effective on the small rodents, frogs and lizards on which it feeds.

Warning coloration

Some species use coloring for exactly the opposite of camouflage: their colors are a very conspicuous advertisement of how dangerous they are. Like the poisonous dart frogs, the coloring of true coral snakes is a warning sign. Predators learn quite quickly that it is better to stay away from any type of coral snake.

Danger!

It's curious that humans use the same colors as nature to warn of danger: yellow, red, black and white. Road signs, hospital signs and symbols for toxic or radioactive materials are good examples of this.

It's not a nest

The bowers are not nests, but invitations for the females, who will select the male with the best and most eye-catching bower. If a female seems interested in his bower, the male offers her a private show in the form of a dance in which he spreads his feathers and shows her brightly-colored objects. If the female likes the male's bower and show, she mates with him and then leaves to build a nest and raise her chicks alone. The male remains in front of his bower and mates with all the females that allow him to do so.

Advertisement

The bowerbird is one of the few cases in the animal world where a construction and its coloring have an exclusively communicative use. Generally, animals build functional structures to serve as shelter (chrysalises, nests, burrows, termite mounds, beehives, etc.) or for hunting (such as spider webs). The bowers are a sort of open-air stage on which the 'artist' performs his theatrical dance in an attempt to enthrall the attending 'audience' (the females).

THEATRICAL ARCHITECTURE

Bowerbirds
Ptilonorhynchidae
Australia and New Guinea

The males of several bird species build bowers (a shelter) by interweaving branches. These are highly spectacular domed structures decorated with all kinds of materials. Each species builds and decorates its bowers differently and often the colors chosen reflect its own coloring. They paint the interior with a mixture of saliva and leaf or berry juice. They also decorate the ground in front of the entrance with stones, bone fragments, shells, flowers, feathers and all sorts of brightly colored objects (even plastic). Once he's finished his construction, the male stays nearby and keeps an eye on it, continuously touching up the smallest details.

BEING THE CENTRE OF ATTENTION

Silvery langur
Trachypithecus cristatus

Malaysia, Sumatra and Borneo

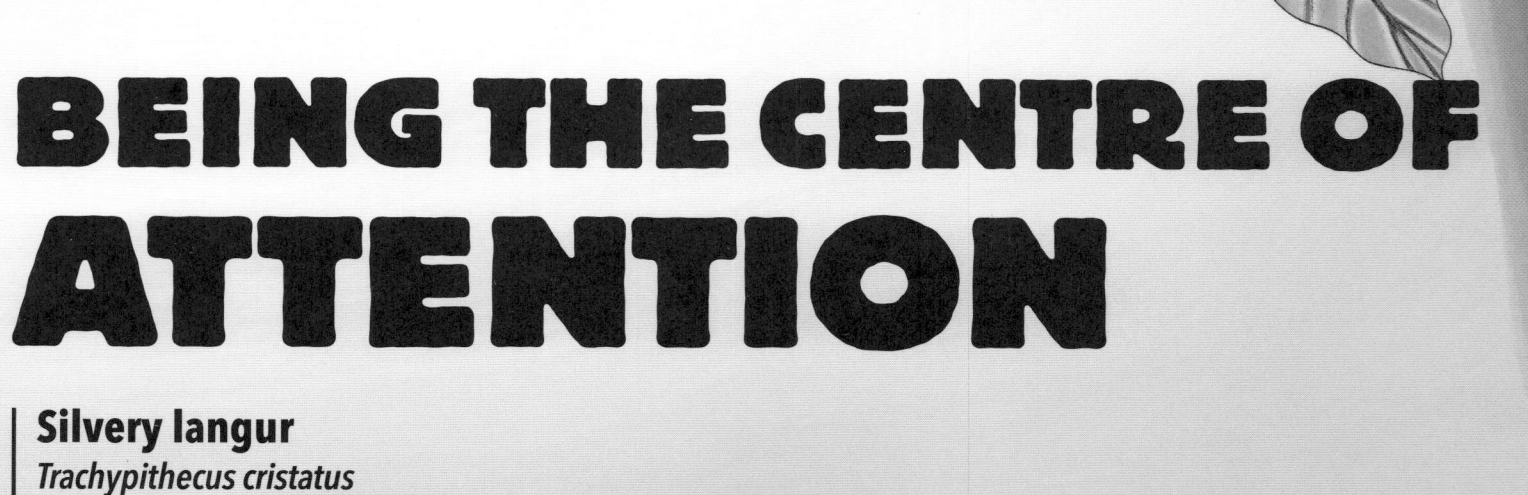

Silvery langurs live in groups of about 20 individuals, consisting of one or two males and several females with their young. Adults are silvery-gray in color, but the young are born bright orange with white facial skin and no fur. This difference serves to make them the center of attention in the group. The mothers often share the care of their young, allowing others to carry and even nurse them. The infants are so attractive that there are sometimes fights to hold them! After half a year, the infant's fur darkens and the group shifts its attention to other, more conspicuous young.

Social learning

Living in social groups allows young primates to pick up the skills essential for survival and life in society, by imitation. This is called social learning and is very common among primates (including our species). Baby langurs learn many of the basic rules for living in the group within six months.

COLORS YOU CAN EAT

Flamingos
Phoenicopterus
Europe, Asia, Africa, Central America and southern South America

Many animals, including mammals, birds and amphibians, cannot synthesize all of the pigments that color their skin or feathers; their coloring comes from food. Flamingos get the pink color of their plumage from eating small red shrimps, which they catch at the bottom of ponds using filtering beaks. These little shrimps cannot manufacture the color red either; they get it from the microscopic algae they eat, which then accumulates in their shells. When a flamingo eats red shrimp, the pigments (carotenoids) are deposited in its growing feathers, which progressively turn pink.

Pigments

The chemicals that lend color to animal tissues are called pigments. The most abundant is melanin, which produces black and brown tones and is found in most living things. Brown colors are the most abundant in nature. Red, yellow and orange colors come from carotenoid pigments, which only plants and algae can produce. Blue or green pigments are rare in animals; these colors are usually achieved by reflection of light on the skin or feathers.

White flamingos?

If we were to eliminate red shrimp from a flamingo's diet, it would gradually lose its coloring and its plumage would end up white. Flamingo chicks are completely white when they hatch from the egg and their parents feed them a pap produced in their digestive tract. It is only after two months that the chicks begin to feed on red shrimps and their color begins to turn pink. But it is not until their fifth year that they reach full pink.

SHINING
WITH THEIR OWN LIGHT

Thousands of species

All over the world, especially in marine waters

On land, it's easy to see things and animals because sunlight illuminates everything. But if you go to the depths of the sea, more than 3280 feet down, it is pitch black. Nevertheless, thousands of species of bacteria, worms, coral, jellyfish, squid, shrimp and fish live there. Three out of four of these species produce their own light to observe their surroundings, hunt prey, scare off predators or find mates. Some light up parts of their bodies, others use luminous antennae, and still others produce bright flashes when attacked.

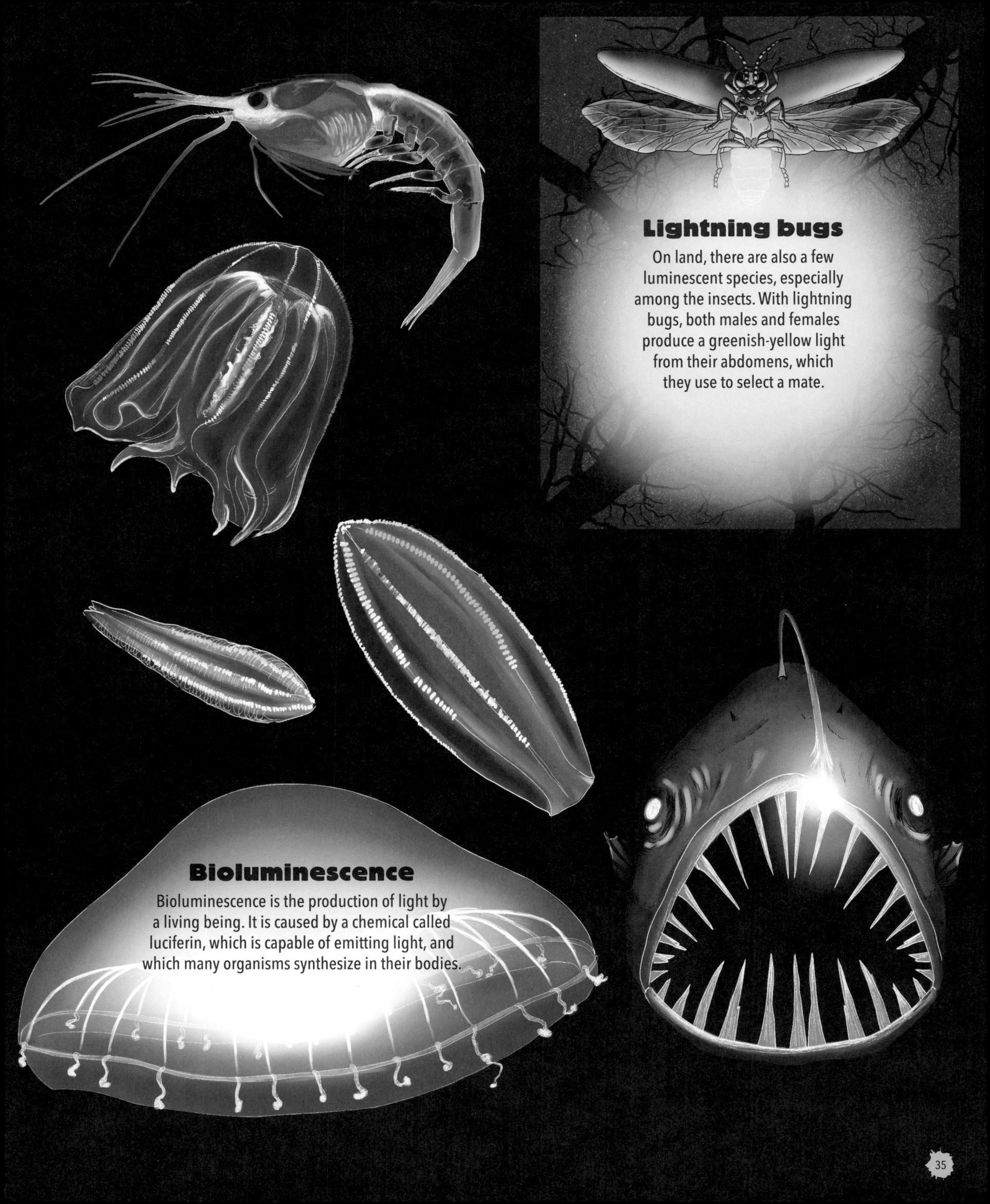

Lightning bugs

On land, there are also a few luminescent species, especially among the insects. With lightning bugs, both males and females produce a greenish-yellow light from their abdomens, which they use to select a mate.

Bioluminescence

Bioluminescence is the production of light by a living being. It is caused by a chemical called luciferin, which is capable of emitting light, and which many organisms synthesize in their bodies.

METAMORPHOSIS IN COLORS

Caterpillars and butterflies
Lepidotera
Throughout the world

Metamorphosis is a phase in the life cycle of butterflies and one of the most fascinating transformation phenomena in nature. All butterflies, both diurnal (daytime) and nocturnal (nighttime) – who are known as moths – were once caterpillars. Butterflies lay eggs and each egg hatches into a caterpillar. After some time, the caterpillar encloses itself in a capsule called a chrysalis, where it undergoes a series of anatomical changes that turn it into a butterfly. Eventually, the butterfly breaks out of the chrysalis and flies away. When it reaches maturity, the butterfly lays eggs and the life cycle begins anew. The caterpillars' colors are very different from those of the butterflies they produce.

Beautiful but dangerous

There are 165,000 species of caterpillar (and their butterflies), an enormous variety in the animal world, second only to beetles (375,000 species). Caterpillars are soft and nutritious, highly palatable to birds, rodents, beetles, wasps, spiders and others. In addition, they move slowly and would be unable to escape an attack. To avoid being eaten, many caterpillars sting or are poisonous and show their danger with colors that act as a warning sign.

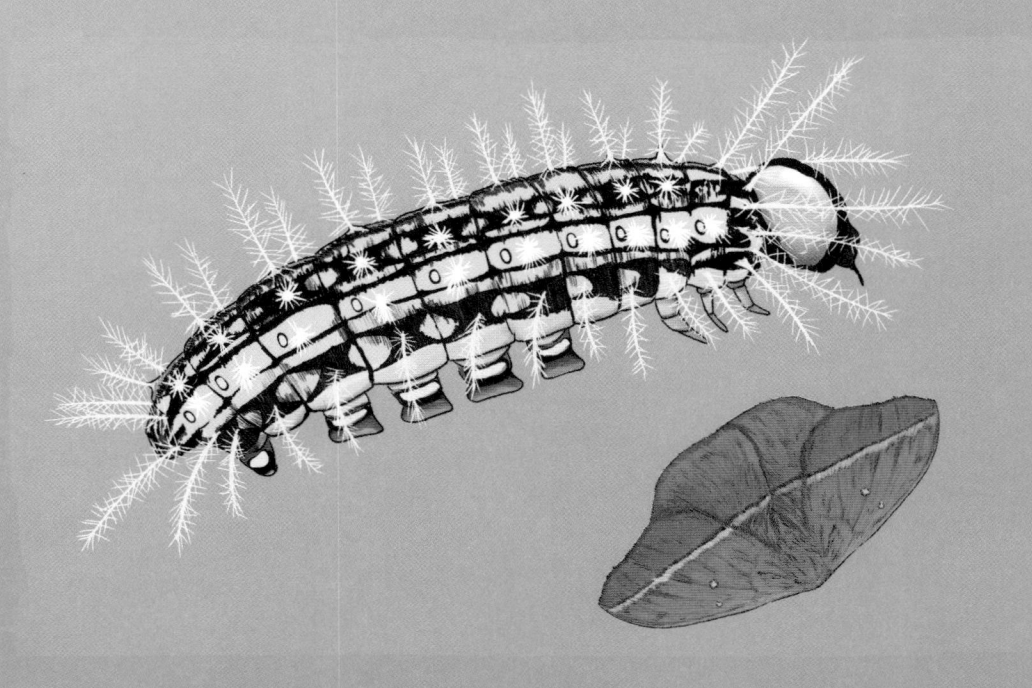

The most poisonous

The caterpillars of the giant silkworm moth of the genus *Lonomia* can cause a serious reaction. In particular, *Lonomia obliqua* can kill a person who has touched it, unless an antidote is administered. The disappearance of wild areas in Brazil and Argentina is leading to an increase of unintentional human contact with these caterpillars.

The more fish, the bluer the legs

Male and female boobies are great fishers of sardines, mackerel, herring and other blue fish. This type of fish is very rich in carotenoid pigment which, after digestion, accumulates in the birds' legs. The more pigment they ingest, the brighter the blue gets.

The boobies' technique consists of catching their prey by surprise, diving with folded wings at about 62 miles per hour into a large shoal. The result is that the better angler an individual is, the better fed it is and therefore the bluer its legs look. If a booby cannot go fishing, its feet start to lose color within a couple of days and its attractiveness fades. On the other hand, as soon as it starts eating fish normally, its legs regain their intense blue color within 48 hours.

LOOK AT MY PRETTY LEGS!

Blue-footed booby
Sula nebouxii

Coastal areas from California to Peru, and the Galapagos Islands

The bluer and brighter the legs, the more attractive blue-footed boobies are to their mates; bright blue denotes good health and guarantees the vigor needed to fish and feed chicks. Males prefer to court the females with the showiest legs. Male boobies give females a stone or a stick and try to impress them by circling around them in a ritual dance in which the most important thing is to proudly display their own blue legs. Suddenly, they spread their wings and raise their beaks to the sky, emitting a distinctive whistling sound. If a female is sufficiently impressed, she starts to follow the male's dance steps, shows her blue feet and repeats the outstretched wing posture as a sign of agreement between the two.

HOW DOES IT CHANGE COLORS?

Panther chameleon
Furcifer pardalis
Madagascar, Mauritius and Réunion

The panther chameleon feeds on a variety of insects. As a slow-moving animal, its hunting tactic is to wait motionless for its victims to approach, and then catch them by shooting out its long, sticky tongue like a bolt of lightning. Chameleons have spectacular colors and are able to change them at will, but it is a misconception that they adapt their colors to their surroundings to camouflage themselves. The male panther chameleon is very territorial and uses its maximum coloring to attract a mate, for example, or threaten other males who enter its terrain. But if it encounters an opponent that seems stronger, it prefers to give up without a fight, quickly showing a discreet dark brown coloring.

A laboratory in the skin

Chameleons are a veritable laboratory for color production thanks to the four reflective layers of their skin. Beneath a first transparent outer layer is a layer of chromatophores, cells containing yellow-red pigments. Beneath this, a layer of transparent, crystalline guanophores reflects blue, creating green colors at will by mixing it with the yellows of the upper layer. The deepest layer contains melanin, the dark pigment we mammals also have, which regulates the amount of light reflected. Chameleons contract or relax these layers and thus manage to freely change their luminous and varied colors.

Independent eyes

The chameleon's eyes can rotate –giving it a full view of its surroundings– and they also move separately, so it can look at two objects at the same time. But when it spots prey, it focuses both eyes on that location and can accurately see an ant several yards away. In addition, chameleons also perceive ultraviolet light, which enriches their visual spectrum.

YUCK! HOW DISGUSTING!

Nudibranchs
Nudibranchia
Marine waters throughout the world

Nudibranchs are gastropod mollusks, relatives of land snails and slugs. Some 3,000 species exist in seas around the world, from the Antarctic all the way through to the Arctic, including tropical waters. Most of them are no more than two inches long and live by crawling on the seafloor, feeding on sponges, corals, gorgonians, fish, squid or cuttlefish eggs, the remains of sea urchins or small crustaceans. All nudibranchs are virtually blind. But surprisingly, many species have some of the most beautiful color combinations in nature.

Two ways of defending themselves

How is it possible that fish and other marine animals don't eat these small, attractive and soft little creatures? Some species use their colors to blend in with their surroundings and go unnoticed, but many others taste foul! Evolution has endowed them with a truly unpleasant taste. Not only that, some species also have stinging and even poisonous appendages. Predators have learned that nudibranchs advertise their bad taste and dangerousness with their wonderful colors and are best left alone.

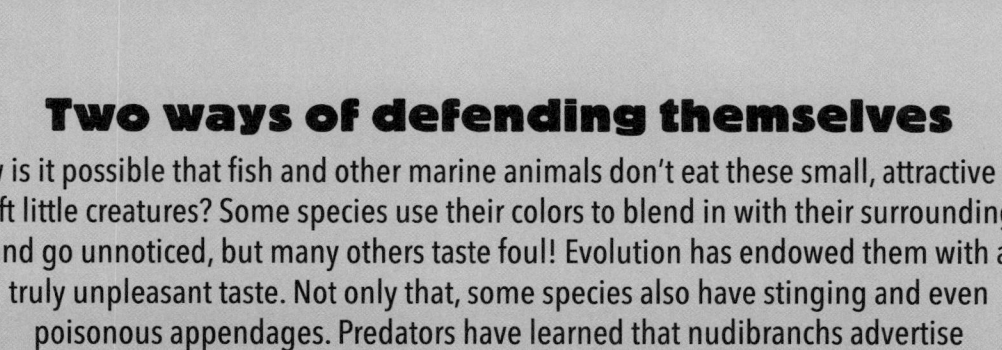

The color green is achieved by combining a yellow pigment with the blue produced by optical effect.

BLUE, AN OPTICAL ILLUSION

Blue is the rarest color in the animal world, because there are no blue pigments that can be manufactured or acquired through diet.

However, many animals manage to appear blue because they have structures in their skin or feathers that produce this color by reflecting light in a certain manner. This way of generating colors through an optical effect is called structural coloration. Combining this effect with pigments creates different colors.